# CLASS 126 DMUs IN SCOTLAND

## THE FIRST INTER CITY UNITS

COLIN J. HOWAT

AMBERLEY

First published 2025

Amberley Publishing
The Hill, Stroud
Gloucestershire, GL5 4EP

www.amberley-books.com



ISBN 978 1 3981 2473 8 (print)
ISBN 978 1 3981 2474 5 (ebook)



British Library Cataloguing in Publication Data.
A catalogue record for this book is available from the British Library.

Typesetting by Hurix Digital, India.
Printed in the UK.

Appointed GPSR EU Representative: Easy Access System Europe Oü, 16879218
Address: Mustamäe tee 50, 10621, Tallinn, Estonia
Contact Details: gpsr.requests@easproject.com, +358 40 500 3575

# Introduction

In 1952 a report commissioned by the British Transport Commission (BTC) on behalf of the government favoured the use of diesel railcars on many routes within Scotland. The Great Western Railway Works at Swindon was chosen to design and build units for the Edinburgh to Glasgow Queen Street High Level line. These sets were to be to a higher 'Inter City' specification as opposed to other designs covering rural lines. The design was to be similar to British Rail Mk1 loco-hauled stock with pullman gangways and buckeye couplings. Intended operation was normally to be in six-car formations. The power cars were to be equipped with two AEC 150-hp underfloor engines with mechanical transmission giving a top speed of 70 mph. These trains had two front end designs. One was with a full-width cab and one was with a half cab with a central gangway connection. The half cab power cars or intermediate vehicles would allow through access for passengers in a six-car set when coupled together. In the power cars, the seating was designed in an open arrangement whilst the trailer coaches were made up of enclosed compartments with side corridors. The class had a unique control air system coded as a white circle, which meant they were incompatible with most other types of Diesel Multiple Units (DMUs). Sixty-four cars including eight buffet cars were built from 1956. Most were introduced onto the Edinburgh to Glasgow Queen Street route but some were sent direct to the Western Region for use.

A second batch of sixty-eight cars were later built between 1959 and 1960 for use on the Glasgow St Enoch to Ayrshire routes. These were closely based on the E&G stock. One major improvement was the moving of the guards van in the power cars to the rear of the coach. This gave the added attraction to passengers of a great forward view of the line ahead behind the driver. The 1956-built cars were allocated to Leith Central, near Edinburgh. They were very intensively used and eventually, after being well worn, replaced on the E&G route from September 1971 by Class 27s and Mk2 stock. Five redundant power cars (DMBSs) were refurbished at Glasgow Works and were exported to Liberia, West Africa, in 1972 for use carrying workers on a mining railway. Four intermediate power cars (DMSLs) were also transferred to Ayr Depot to join the second batch. The Ayrshire fleet grinded on until the final sets were withdrawn from service in January 1983. The first series numbered 79xxx vehicles were introduced in January 1957 between Edinburgh and Glasgow Queen Street including services via Falkirk Grahamston. The usual formation on the E&G services was six cars with the half cab intermediate power cars positioned in the middle coupled up. The full-width cabs could not be coupled up to each other as no through electrical connections had been provided. The Ayrshire sets were numbered in the 51xxx range and provided with full electrical connections in all power cars, so it was not uncommon for two Motor Brake Second (DMBs) vehicles to be coupled up together. By the late 1970s, the first-class compartments in the trailer cars were downgraded to second class. The front-end gangway connections were also welded up between 1979 and 1981 due to drivers complaining of bad draughts.

The 126s had a monopoly of the Stranraer/Ayr to Glasgow Central passenger services until the early 1980s when more Class 101 and 107 sets began to appear. In February 1981, 79088 and 79470 were the first 126s to be officially withdrawn from Ayr Depot and were observed laid up in Falkland Yard. Later in August, 51041, 51045, 59405 and 51019 were also taken out of service. From October 1981 there were still fifteen sets in traffic but more Class 101s and 107s started to arrive at Ayr Depot. The next major change was from May 1982. Hamilton Depot had closed and the remaining Class 107 sets were all transferred to Ayr Depot. With the added addition of Class 26/27s working the majority of the Glasgow to Stranraer Harbour services, the writing was on the wall for the 126s. By the beginning of October, only four sets remained in traffic and two of these were withdrawn at the end of that month. This left only 406 and 413 sets in traffic. On Saturday 9 October 1982 the Swindon Diesel Preservation Society (SDPS) organised a farewell railtour along many Ayrshire branch lines. This included Hunterston Low Level, Troon Avoiding Line, Killoch Colliery and the Chalmerston branch. It eventually headed back up in the dark to Elderslie where it reversed and ran to Kilmacolm. After a short stay it headed back to Central via Paisley Canal. From November 1982, these two remaining sets, 406 and 413, still appeared on Ayr and Largs services and the odd Kilmacolm working. In late November I travelled up to Largs in 413 set. After taking some pictures, I was met by the driver taking the set back to Central and was given the opportunity to drive it to Kilwinning in 51017! By the start of 1983, the end was near and with the shortsighted closure of the Kilmacolm branch, time was almost out. My final journey was in 51036 on 20 January 1983 on the 16.00 Central to Ayr. A few days later both 406 and 413 units were hauled from Ayr Depot to Dunfermline Townhill by a pair of Class 20s to await their future. By March 1983 I set off to Dunfermline Townhill Depot to see my old friends. I arrived on a quiet Saturday morning and it was an eerie feeling like being in a time warp. By this time I had joined the SDPS and it was later arranged for myself to take four lifting brackets from Ayr Depot to assist with the lifting of the preserved unit 413 at Laurencekirk onto low loaders for the trip to the Caledonian Preservation Group at Brechin. Eventually both sets were taken to Thornton Yard at the end of May 1983. Unit 413 was bound for Laurencekirk Sidings and 406 was taken back to Ayr Depot for asset stripping, although fitters from Haymarket Depot had already taken out the engines from both power cars 51036 and 51026.

The earlier 1956 126s from their initial arrival at Leith Depot worked mainly on the Edinburgh to Glasgow Queen Street via Falkirk High and Grahamston services. They also worked over the Waverley route when they were delivered from Swindon to Leith and occasionally on local services around Edinburgh. They also worked from Queen Street Low Level via Anniesland and Airdrie to Edinburgh during engineering work. A demonstration six-car set had already worked to Ayr in November 1958 to give staff and passengers a foretaste of the second batch of 126s to come. The Ayr-based sets worked from St Enoch to Ayr and Stranraer Harbour, later switching to Central in June 1966. However, they also worked to Ardrossan Harbour, Largs, Kilbarchan Loop Line, Barassie to Kilmarnock, Dalry to Kilmarnock, the Dalmellington Branch, Heads of Ayr, Barrhead to Carlisle via Kilmarnock, Paisley Canal, East Kilbride, Kilmarnock to Darvel and the Gourock line. In the summer of 1959 and until the full Ayrshire services were introduced in November, some of the Ayr sets were sent to Leith Depot and worked between Edinburgh and Queen Street High Level. This included 51011 as part of a four-car set. This consisted of 79100, 59532, 51011 and 79102. Other sightings on the E&G services included 51008, 59392 and 51009 at Queen Street on 24 July 1959. The late 1950s and early 1960s were big events for young train spotters at Aberdeen due to the Glasgow Fair holidays when west coast families travelled by train to Aberdeen. This brought unusual steam workings and also sightings of brand-new DMUs based in the Glasgow area. This included the Inter City sets. Noted as visiting Aberdeen were 51012/13, 51030/31/32/33/35/37/38/39/40/41, 59391/95/96/97/98 and 59402/04/05.

Both 126 batches worked over the West Highland lines on tourist excursions in the mid-1960s and they also worked specials to the Lake District and Blackpool North. An old friend, Willie Carlyle, based at Ayr Depot advised me that due to occasional railbus failures in the early 1960s, 126s worked between Irvine and Kilmarnock and also between Kilmarnock and Darvel. In May 1969 a Branch Line Society Railtour called the 'Tam O' Shanter' took a three-car set all over Ayrshire including the Kilbarchan Loop, Muirkirk and also ran between Dalry and Kilmarnock. In August 1981 I had obtained a Freedom of Scotland ticket and joined a six-car 126 at Irvine on the 15.05 Stranraer Harbour to Central working. On arrival at Central, the sets were booked to go empty coaches (ECS) to Corkerhill Depot. However, a railman advised me that they were in fact stepping onto a Shotts working due to a 107 failure. I cancelled my next move, stayed at Central and had a great journey to Shotts and back. In fact the driver and guard allowed me to stay on the set and we worked out ECS to Benhar Junction. We then reversed and went back to Shotts to form a service to Motherwell where the train terminated. From September 1979 the gangway vestibules began to be removed due to draughts. Around the same time, the guards compartments in the DMBSs power cars were modified to include a partition, again to reduce draughts. By September 1983 the last 126s left Falkland Yard, Ayr, and were moved south via Mauchline and Dumfries to the furnaces at Snailwell in Ely, Cambridgeshire. Some were parked up at Carlisle Kingmoor and various other English yards until they could be accepted. However, by the end of 1984 most had been incinerated – the end of an era.

## Friends' Recollections

A late friend of my father, Joe McSwiggan, who worked with BR, travelled frequently between Irvine and Glasgow. Joe recalled that on 2 November 1959 the new 126 service came into operation. That morning he boarded the 07.45 Ayr to St Enoch. The leading power car was 51045. The next day it was 51047, then 51031, 51036 and 51030 on the Friday. The units were fantastic and a lot warmer than the old steam carriages. Joe also described another incident. Travelling on the 17.10 St Enoch to Ayr in a nine-car set, it departed from Kilwinning with all engines revving, when a pin stripe-suited businessman leapt up out of his seat, grabbed his suitcase and coat from the luggage rack and rushed to the exit door. However, it was too late to alight as the train was going too fast for him, so he settled down again until Irvine and presumably caught the next northbound service home. This was a scene too familiar to Joe as the improved heated 126 sets seemed to have a great somnolent effect on passengers returning home from work. Enthusiast Lou Wilson from Glasgow stated that he first came across the spirit of the Class 126s as a wee boy of six around Easter 1960 when family Wilson took a day trip to Troon. At St Enoch in place of the expected compartment steam train, there was a green 126. These sets looked the part. The seats were high backed and comfortable and you could choose between the open coaches of the power cars or the compartments of the trailer coaches. He left St Enoch, ran via Paisley Canal onto Elderslie and instead of taking the main line to Johnstone, the service was routed towards Cart Junction and then onto the North Johnstone Line. That took them via Kilbarchan and Kilbirnie and he remembers the clicky click of the old jointed track all the way to Dalry. In addition to the heavy commuter traffic from many stations, thousands of Glaswegians would buy cheap day returns and evening tickets to the coast. On summer Saturdays and during the race meetings at Bogside or Ayr, additional sets would be made up. The Stranraer and Girvan services were usually worked by three cars, with certain workings up to six cars in the summer months and even nine cars during the Glasgow Fair.

As well as the 79xxx buffet cars, Ayr Depot directly received some of the ex-Western Region intermediate power cars. Sandy Logan stated he was also a regular traveller during the 1960s. Late one winter's evening in 1965, he was seated on the 21.55 St Enoch to Ayr service when the driver spotted him as he walked to his cab. The driver said to Sandy, 'If you fancy comin' up the front just wait till wur oot the station and I'll leave the door unlocked. The'll be nae Inspectors once were oot on the City Union and the gairds ah reeght.' This driver called Jimmy stated to Sandy, 'Dae ye ken how tae stop these units without a rug? Watch me at the next stop.' In layman's terms, Jimmy meant how to stop the train smoothly without a jolt. Jimmy also stated that the 79xxx cars were trouble. On the other hand, the public loved them and many sought them out to travel in. Their heaters were brilliantly death valley in effect. He also stated, 'There's nae intermediate setting on the heater controls – it was full on or nothing. If the passenger saloons were cauld – you baled oot!'

An early shot of an E&G 79 DMBS power car under construction at Swindon Works. (January 1956/British Railways)

A completed 79 DMBS power car at Swindon Works. Note the guards van behind the driver's compartment. This was redesigned on the Ayrshire fleet and moved to the rear on the later batches. (August 1956/British Railways)

Power car 79095 just recently constructed at Swindon Works. Note the curtains provided. (January 1956/British Railways)

Trailer coach 59393 at Swindon Works. This was made for part of the Ayr depot allocation. (April 1959/British Railways)

An interior staged view inside a trailer buffer coach. This was a promotional shot probably taken at Swindon Works or at a local station. (August 1956/British Railways)

An interior shot of DMSL 79157 at Swindon Works prior to working in passenger traffic. The E&G motor brake coaches differed from their Ayrshire counterparts as there was no middle internal or external passenger doors, just a partition between compartments. (July 1956/British Railways)

*Left*: A view inside the cab of a Driving Motor Brake Second Cab (DMBS) of the original 79xxx series of coaches. (July 1956/British Railways)

*Below*: Two early Class 126 sets at Edinburgh Princes Street station. On the left a service to Glasgow Central via Shotts and on the right a service for Lanark via Carstairs. (August 1965/ Brian Haslehust)

A typical scene at Ayr station sees a six-car set making a smokey departure whilst another three-car set lies in the bay platform. (October 1979)

A six-car set at Edinburgh departing with a service to Queen Street. This was taken from a BR publicity postcard. (May 1957/British Railways)

A six-car set at Queen Street, DMBS 79109 with a service to Edinburgh via Falkirk Grahamston. Note the sidings to the right. These were removed during the electrification project in 2016. (January 1957/David Kay)

DMSL 51012 arrives at Dundee at the head of a six-car special returning from Aberdeen to Queen Street. The Ayrshire DMUs were drafted in during the Glasgow Fair holidays to assist with the movement of heavy passenger loadings. Note the headcode panels were covered up by stencil-lettered boards. These would be removed when the sets started running on the Ayrshire services. (July 1960/British Railways)

A view of the old St Enoch station from the hotel side. The Swindons ran here from 1959 until 1966. In June 1966, all services were transferred to Central. At that time there was capacity – sixty years on Central is reaching bursting point and the St Enoch Shopping Centre is to be replaced by new offices. Yet again no forward transport planning as we head towards the 2030s. (March 1965/British Railways)

A three-car set on the Troon Avoiding Line with a St Enoch to Stranraer Harbour express. This line was closed as part of the Ayrshire Electrification Project in November 1982. Interestingly the two power cars are DMBS coaches. (July 1963/Hector McSporran)

*Left*: A three-car set emerges into Princes Street Gardens, Edinburgh, with a service to Queen Street. Note the front whiskers had been replaced by a yellow warning panel. (August 1966/David Kay)

*Below*: A six-car set approaches Polmont with an Edinburgh to Queen Street service. Note the second coach from the rear was still in green livery. (April 1968/ David Kay)

An E&G set in blue and white livery stands at the buffers at Queen Street in company with a Class 27. Note the advert above the platform and the platform ticket machines below the arrival board. (August 1968/David Kay)

A three-car set at Dumfries with a Carlisle to Ayr service. The middle road was removed in the early 1990s. (December 1979)

A six-car set arrives at Barassie with a St Enoch to Ayr service. Note the front three cars were from the 51xxx series and the rear three were from the 79xxx series. The station staff seemed to be in a hurry! (July 1960/Angus Ross)

A six-car set at platform 5 Central. These units were unusually used on a Shotts working due to the failure of a Class 107 unit. (August 1981)

A three-car set in the snow at Hairmyres with a St Enoch to East Kilbride service. The 126s were rarely used on this line and usually only when there was a shortage of Class 100, 101,107 or 116 sets. (February 1964/Hamish Stevenston)

Queen Street station. On the left a Class 2 service for Edinburgh via Falkirk Grahamston and on the right a Class 1 service for Edinburgh via Falkirk High. (May 1970/David Kay)

A six-car set departs Edinburgh with a service to Queen Street. Leading car was 79088. This was one of the last to be painted into the blue and white livery. It was then transferred to Ayr Depot in September 1971 and repainted into rail blue. It was again repainted back to the blue and white livery in March 1978. (April 1970/David Kay)

A six-car set approaches Airdrie with a diverted Queen Street Low Level to Edinburgh service. It is believed that this service had been diverted due to the Castlecary crash involving DMBS 79092. (September 1968/Brian Haslehust)

A six-car set crosses the River Ayr on approach to the station with a service from St Enoch. (May 1961/Angus Ross)

A three-car set at Heads of Ayr with a service to Central. This station provided access to the nearby Butlins Camp. However, it was still closed by Dr Beeching. (April 1968/Angus Ross)

A six-car set unusually with a DMSL power car leading in Princes Street Gardens, Edinburgh, with a service from Queen Street. (April 1968/David Kay)

The Castlecary accident. Due to a mix-up between signalman and driver, a Class 25 rammed into the rear of an E&G set working between Queen Street and Edinburgh. Extensive damage was sustained to DMBS 79092, which was withdrawn from service. (September 1968/ British Railways)

A six-car set at Garrowhill Halt with a test train from Queen St Low Level to Edinburgh via Airdrie and Bathgate. This was prior to the full introduction onto the E&G line shortly afterwards. This station was renamed Garrowhill when the line was electrified in 1961. (October 1956/Paul Strathdee)

A six-car set near Crookston with an Ayr to St Enoch working. Note the full headcode in use. This line is now singled and only runs as far as Paisley Canal. (April 1965/Angus Ross)

Brand-new Class 126 trailers lying stabled at Lugton Sidings. They had been delivered a few days earlier and were waiting to be taken to Ayr Depot and formed into sets. The leading vehicle appears to be 59407. (September 1959/Angus Ross)

A six-car set on the fast line passes Hillington West with a St Enoch to Ayr service. This area was reduced to two tracks shortly after this photo was taken but went back to three tracks in 2012. (April 1966/Angus Ross)

A six-car set departs St Enoch with a service to Ayr via Kilbrachan. Note the fireman sitting behind the left window. It took until the early 1970s for this over manning to be accepted by ASLEF and finally withdrawn. (March 1961/Angus Ross)

A three-car set arrives at Thorntonhall with a service from St Enoch to East Kilbride. This branch opened up to electrics from December 2025. (September 1964/Hamish Stevenston)

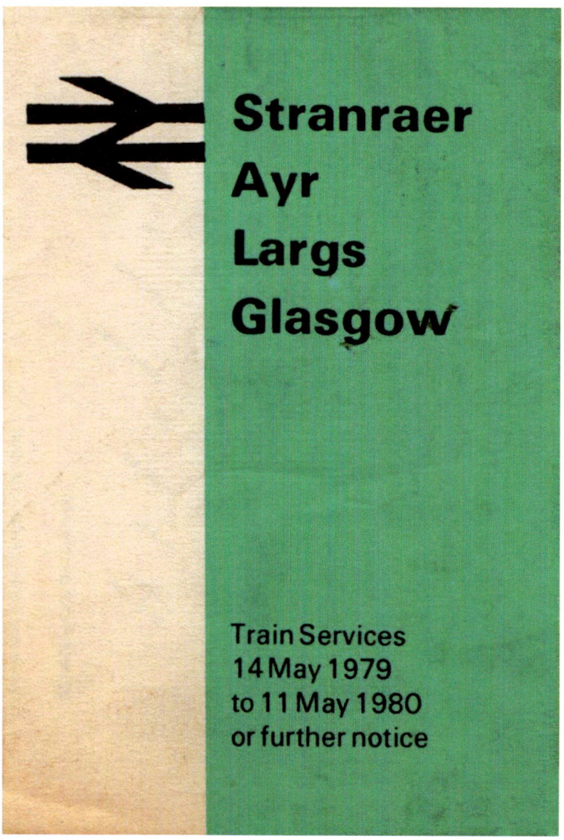
Stranraer
Ayr
Largs
Glasgow

Train Services
14 May 1979
to 11 May 1980
or further notice

*Above*: A three-car set at Dalmellington, with 50936 trailing. Normally this service was worked by a railbus. However, on this day it had failed and the three-car 126 was utilised instead. (March 1964/Angus Ross)

*Left*: The front cover of a BR pocket timetable from 1979 to 1980. (British Rail)

A three-car set departs Central with the 10.35 service to Ayr, 51038 leading. Note the car park in the background. (October 1979)

A six-car set passes the site of Monkton station near Prestwick with a Central to Ayr service. The sidings on the left are still in use for the supply of aviation fuel to the airport. (November 1969/ Angus Ross)

A Class 126 shares St Enoch with a Class 107 Derby unit. Going by the headcode the 126 would appear to be working an East Kilbride service. This was the last day of official operations and the next day all services were transferred to Central. (June 1966/Angus Ross)

A six-car set north of Irvine with an Ayr to Central service, 51039 leading. The flats, like the units, are long gone, being demolished by 2023. (June 1980)

A six-car set departs Glasgow Buchanan Street with a diverted service to Edinburgh. Queen Street had been closed due to engineering work. This was the last day of operation from this station. Note the building in the background in the process of being constructed. This was to become Buchanan House and was the base of BR Scottish operations from 1967. (November 1966/Brian Haslehust)

A six-car set passes through Airdrie station with a diverted Queen Street Low Level to Edinburgh service. Note the Blue trains stabled in the adjacent platform. (September 1968/Brian Haslehust)

A six-car set at Pinwherry with a Stranraer Harbour to St Enoch service. This station was closed in September 1965. (March 1962/Angus Ross)

A three-car set at the south end bay platform at Ayr. It was working services between Ayr and Heads of Ayr. This was one of the sets sent direct to Ayr from the Western Region in 1960 before moving onto Leith Depot. The leading car was 79085. (May 1966/Angus Ross)

A six-car set between Prestwick and Newton-on-Ayr with a St Enoch to Girvan service. (March 1962/Angus Ross)

A three-car set arrives at Barassie, with 51035 leading an Ayr to Central service. The Troon Avoiding Line was removed in 1983 and this area has been completely transformed since electrification. (June 1979)

A six-car set departing Central with a service to Ayr. Note the slight damage on the right-hand side of the cab and the headcode still in use. (April 1976/Angus Ross)

A nine-car set heading into Central with a morning peak-hour service from Ayr. Note the third last coach in blue and white livery. It is thought that this was ex-E&G coach 79165, which had been sent to Ayr after 51011 was destroyed in the Gower Street accident in 1973. (March 1974/Angus Ross)

A three-car set at the closed Kilbirnie station on the North Johnstone Line. The set was working a railtour named the 'Tam O' Shanter'. This was another useful diversionary route but local traffic ceased with the closure of St Enoch in June 1966. It continued to be used as a diversionary route until June 1972. (May 1969/Angus Ross)

The E&G 126 cars occasionally visited Central usually during engineering works. Here we see a DMBS trailing as part of a six-car set departing with a service to Edinburgh. (February 1969/David Kay)

A six-car E&G set departs Queen Street with a service for Edinburgh, with power car 79090 leading. (May 1970/David Kay)

A three-car set at Girvan with a service to Ayr. Note the set was still in original green livery but the whiskers had been replaced by a yellow warning panel. (June 1964/Hector McSporran)

The ill-fated 51011 being lifted by a crane at Gower Street near Shields Junction. This was struck by a 303 Blue Train and caught fire and was completely destroyed. It was cut up on site and later replaced by 79165 ex-Millerhill. However, 79165 also had electrical problems and was replaced by 79168. (August 1973/unknown newspaper)

A six-car set at Paisley Gilmour Street with the 17.25 Glasgow Central to Stranraer Harbour service. Note the set No. 120 in the left leading window, the headcode, the first class and the BRUTES for moving parcels, all now sadly but a memory. (June 1974/Angus Ross)

A six-car set passes Ayr Depot with an Ayr to Central service. The rear power car has the unit No. 126410, indicating that this was MSL coach No. 51013. (September 1981)

A three-car set near Shotts with a Glasgow Central to Edinburgh service on a typical snowy day. (January 1965/Brian Haslehust)

79109 withdrawn from traffic and a partner at Millerhill Yard. It was taken out of service in September 1971 and was finally cut up at Snailwell, Cambridgeshire, by January 1982. (April 1973/David Kay)

A three-car set arrives at Kingsknowe with an Edinburgh to Central via Shotts service. At this time, 126s were fairly rare on this route. (April 1968/David Kay)

A three-car set departs Stranraer Town with ECS being shunted probably to the Harbour station after arriving on a local service from Ayr. (August 1964/Brian Haslehust)

A side view of an Ayr-based Motor Brake Second Power Car, 51038. It was on the rear of the 10.45 Ayr to Central service just north of Irvine station. (November 1977)

A six-car set east of Arkleston Junction between Paisley Gilmour Street and Central with an Ayr to Central service. The front coach had just received the new blue and white livery. (September 1977)

A six-car set in the snow north of Kilwinning with an Ayr to Central working. Note the signal box and station in the background. (February 1980)

A six-car set approaches Glengarnock signal box with a Central to Ayr service. Note the old Caledonian bridge abutments above the box. This was the branch from Giffen to Kilbirnie South station, which was closed to passengers in December 1930. (June 1982)

Trailer coach 59400 at Ayr depot in between duties. Note the yellow band indicating that the first-class compartments were still in use. These were phased out from late 1977, although the seating still remained. They also had two toilets and by this time partial no smoking compartments had been introduced. (April 1976/Hamish McSporran)

*Right*: A close-up of a Driving Motor Second Leading (DMSL) coach gangway at Central platform 11. It had just arrived on a service from Ayr. (July 1976)

*Below*: A six-car set arrives at Newton-on-Ayr with a Central to Ayr service. Note the railman coming out to meet the train. Newton-on-Ayr was unstaffed from the mid-1980s and the station building behind the railman is now part of an undertakers! (October 1979)

A three-car set passes over the A78 bypass on the outskirts of Kilwinning with a Girvan to Central service. Note the old semaphore signals controlled by Byrehill signal box, which was just out of the picture to the left. (May 1982)

Power car 51031 stabled in between duties at Ayr Depot. This coach was unfortunately destroyed in the Paisley Gilmour Street collision when the train it was leading passed a signal at danger resulting in it being struck by a six-car 303. (May 1977)

The aftermath of the Paisley Gilmour Street crash. 51031 was badly damaged, as was the leading coach of the 303 set. 51031 was moved a mile up the track to Arkleston Junction and cut up on site. (April 1979/unknown newspaper)

A six-car set comes off the Troon Avoiding Line at Lochgreen Junction with the morning Central to Stranraer Harbour service. At this time this was the only booked passenger service over the route. This useful route was short-sightedly removed by the engineers in November 1982. (April 1980)

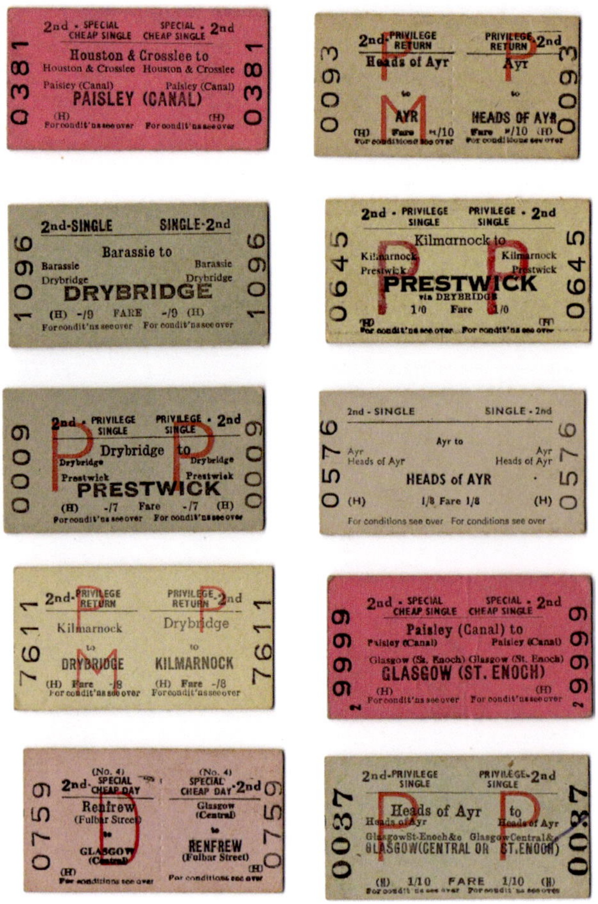


*Above*: A six-car set arrives at Dalry with a Central to Stranraer Harbour service. Note the slow lines. These were cut back to Swinlees as part of the electrification project in 1986. (July 1979)

*Left*: Some samples of the different types of tickets available to the public. Note the old fares and many of the destinations are sadly no longer available to the travelling public. (May 2024)

An internal view of MBS 51045 near Maybole. These views made travelling great unless the driver put the blind down. (July 1979)

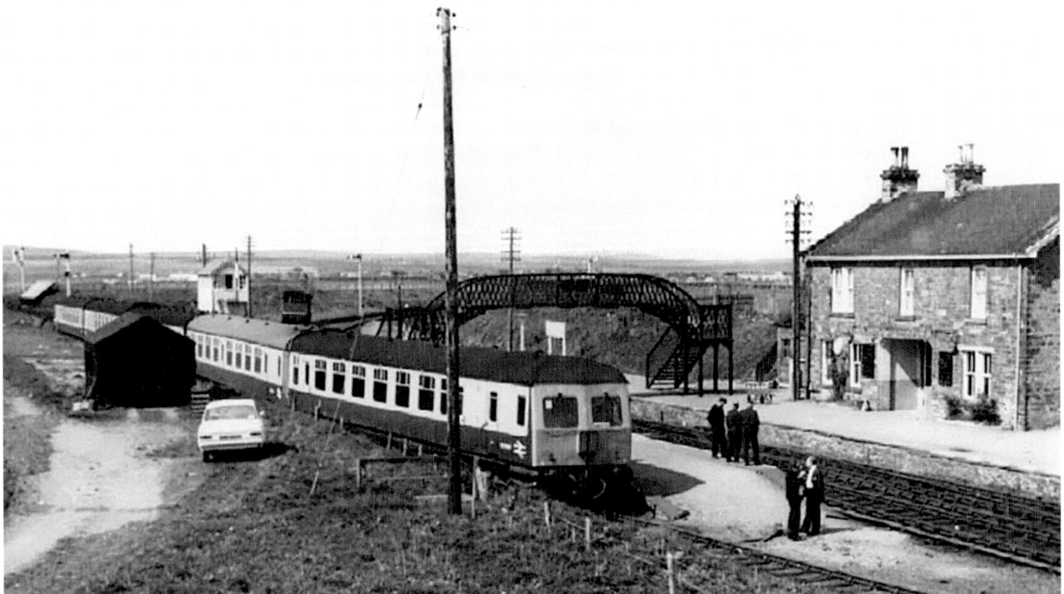

Five-car ex-E&G 126 at Georgemas Junction. After being displaced from the E&G lines, an experiment was tried out with this set to see if it was viable on the far north lines. The train also included a buffet vehicle. However, BR concluded that the testing was not successful and they were never used in passenger service on these lines. (April 1972/Hamish Stevenston)

08430 (AY) assists with the lifting of power car 51032 (AY) at Ayr depot. The coach had just been fitted with new wheelsets. (September 1981)

A six-car set in the snow at Kilwinning, with 51040 leading. One good thing about the Swindons was that you could usually rely on their heaters in the winter! (February 1980)

A six-car set arriving at Kilwinning, with 79088 leading. Note the old headcode boxes with Nos 1 and 2 at the front. Upgraded headcode blinds were never added into these coaches. It was working the 15.35 Central to Ayr service. (June 1977)

A six-car set approaches Fairlie High station and signal box with the 'Ayrshire Wanderer' railtour. It was heading to Largs before moving south to other branch lines. (October 1982)

A three-car set arrives at Kilwinning, with 51048 leading a Central to Ayr service. The sub Class 126 identification numbers on the front were later added from around 1980. (July 1979)

A six-car set in the jungle outside Central with a Central to Ayr service, with 79168 trailing. Note the paint marks on the roof possibly caused by vandals. (August 1977)

A three-car set at the north end of Falkland Yard with the 09.10 Ayr to Carlisle service. This service ran from May 1979 until September 1982. (November 1979)

A typical scene at Ayr station with the Class 126s. Two sets tie up in platform 3. Note DMSL 51027 stabled behind in platform 2. (October 1979)

A six-car set passes Bogside Racecourse signal box with an Ayr to Central service. The box was renamed simply Bogside from 1978. Bogside Racecourse used to share the Scottish Grand Nationals until the mid-1960s when Ayr Racecourse took over completely. (May 1977)

A six-car set on the Hunterston Low Level Branch connecting line with the 'Ayrshire Wanderer' railtour. It was returning to Hunterston High Level Junction and worked to Largs where the sets were split and reversed. (October 1982)

A six-car set north of Irvine with an Ayr to Central service, 51041 leading. Irvine had two stations. However, the Caledonian station at Bank Street situated nearer the town centre closed in 1933. (October 1979)

Former preserved trailer coach 79441 at the Strathspey railway in Aviemore. After withdrawal in 1972 it spent twenty years at Aviemore and was named *Glenfiddich*. However, due to the costs of removing asbestos it was scrapped at Glasgow Works by October 1992. (May 1988)

A six-car set arrives at Ayr with a Central to Girvan service, 51051 leading. The flats in the background were built in the late 1960s. (October 1979)

A six-car set approaches platform 13 Central with a service from Ayr. Note the 311 set departing probably on a Wemyss Bay or Gourock service. (May 1973/Angus Ross)

79168 lying withdrawn at Ayr Depot. It was only in the blue and white livery for about two months when it was taken out of traffic in May 1978 due to asbestos problems. It was quickly cannibalised and disposed of by March 1980. (August 1978)

A six-car set at Swinlees north of Dalry with a morning peak service from Ayr to Central. These tracks were reduced from four to two at this point as part of the electrification project in 1986. (April 1980)

A three-car set arrives at Barassie with an Ayr to Central service, 51044 leading. Note the old AA bus in the background. (December 1981)

Trailer coach 79479 at Ayr station. This was initially sent to Ayr Depot for part of the Ayrshire fleet. It was later moved to Leith Depot around 1965. It then returned to Ayr in 1968 and was withdrawn from traffic in 1981. (May 1977)

A three-car set passes Mosspark with a diverted Girvan to Central service. This was due to a points failure at Paisley Gilmour Street. Note the staff changing posters at the booking office. (November 1980)

A six-car set passes Howwood signal box with a Central to Ayr service. Howwood station was reopened just behind the camera position in March 2001. (December 1979)

A six-car set crosses Campbells Brig Viaduct near Irvine in the snow with an Ayr to Central service, 51016 leading. (February 1980)

Ayr Depot as we like to remember it. This five-car set had 51015 at the north end. One wonders what it was like on a typical nightshift with AEC engines revving up and smoke galore! (September 1981)

*Above*: A three-car set north of Kilwinning with a Girvan to Central working. Note the engineers wagons to the right and the signal box just beyond the rear coach. (June 1980)

*Right*: A three-car set at Barassie with the 14.00 Carlisle to Ayr service. This is one of the journeys that I enjoyed the most – 70 mph virtually all the way from Dumfries to Kilmarnock. Despite being sensible, the Kilmarnock platform has never been reintroduced since closure in 1969. (September 1980)

A six-car set arrives at Ayr with a Girvan to Central service, 51019 leading. This power car was one of the early casualties, being withdrawn in July 1981. (October 1979)

A three-car set, with 51037 leading, arrives at Crookston with a Kilmacolm to Central service. This route is still open but mainly single and only as far as Paisley Canal. (September 1982/ Hamish Stevenston)

A side view of MBS 51036 near Irvine working an Ayr to Central service. (November 1977)

A six-car set at Paisley Gilmour Street, with 51013 trailing on an Ayr to Central service. This is the location in April 1979 where the guard belled the driver of an Ayr to Central relief service to depart but the signal at the end of the platform was at red. This resulted in a six-car set colliding with a six-car Blue train from Central to Wemyss Bay. Unfortunately it resulted in the death of both drivers and five passengers, with sixty-eight injured. (July 1980)

A three-car set at platform 12 Central after arrival on a service from Ayr. Note EMU 311110 of Shields Depot in platform 13. (September 1980)

A six-car set at Brownhill Junction south of Glengarnock with a Sunday Central to Ayr service, 51046 leading. Note the Kilbarchan Flyover in the background. This bridge was removed in 1986. (March 1981)

A six-car set east of Airdrie with a diverted Queen Street Low Level to Edinburgh service. This was diverted due to engineering works and was about to pass the former Calderbank Iron Works. (May 1968/Brian Haslehust)

A six-car set at Ayr in complete all-blue livery on a service to Central, 51042 leading. This was in the middle of another great hot summer. Where have these summers gone? (June 1976/Hamish McSporran)

*Above*: A three-car set north of Irvine with an Ayr to Central working, 51035 leading. The grass area beyond the boundary wall had two sidings for the storing of wagons for the nearby ICI complex at Ardeer. (September 1980)

*Left*: Four car at Kilwinning with additional DMSL 51023 at the front. Very unusual as most formations were three-, six- or nine-car sets. This formation may have been to test out 51023 for engine checks. (February 1981)

A three-car set at Stranraer Harbour having just arrived with a service from Glasgow Central. Note the goods and parcels vehicles. This station is now a shadow of its former self. (July 1972/ Brian Haslehust)

A six-car set in the snow north of Kilwinning with a Girvan to Central working. The sidings on the right were taken out of use in 2015. (February 1980)

*Above*: A six-car set at Ardrossan South Beach with an Ardrossan Winton Pier to Central working. This platform was removed as part of the remodelling during the electrification project in 1987, although the track remains for freight only and is still causing major congestion. (November 1982)

*Left*: A six-car set climbs Dailly Bank near Maybole with a Central to Stranraer Harbour service. This was a mixture of E&G and Ayrshire sets. Formation was 79088, 79470, 79168, 51015, 59397 and 51045. (May 1977/ Angus Ross)

A six-car set departs Central platform 11 with a service to Girvan, 51039 leading. The car park is long gone but rail capacity has improved little. (August 1979)

A three-car set at Girvan with a service to Central, with 51042 trailing. The line between Girvan and Dalrymple Junction was singled in 1974 with a crossing Loop at Kilkerran. (August 1981)

A six-car set near Waterside station on the Chalmerston branch with the 'Ayrshire Wanderer' railtour. The guard appears to be rather bemused at his surroundings. Class 126s did travel over this branch previously in passenger and other railtour workings. (October 1982)

A nine-car set at Arkleston Junction with a Stranraer Harbour to Central service, 51044 leading. The siding in the foreground was the last remnant of the old Renfrew Wharf branch. (July 1979)

A three-car set at Kilmarnock departs with the 14.00 Carlisle to Ayr service. The Mk1 stock was stabled in the middle road awaiting Celtic football supporters coming back from Rugby Park for the return to Central. (December 1979)

A six-car set at Dalry with an Ayr to Central service, 51035 leading. The four platforms were reduced to two and the overbridge completely replaced during the electrification project in 1986. (July 1979)

*Above*: A six-car set passes Ayr No. 1 signal box with a Girvan to Central service, 51038 leading. (August 1981)

*Left*: A three-car set at Lochside with a Central to Ayr service. This station was renamed Lochwinnoch on commencement of the Ayrshire electrification project from September 1986. (December 1979)

A six-car set at Paisley Gilmour Street, with 51044 trailing. It was working a Central to Girvan service. (July 1979)

Three-car set at Kilmarnock having just arrived with the 10.35 ex-Stranraer Harbour, with 51042 trailing. This service connected in with a loco-hauled train from Central to Carlisle. (February 1982)

*Above*: A six-car set passes Byrehill Junction south of Kilwinning with the 08.35 Central to Stranraer Harbour service. The line in the foreground leads to Dubbs Junction and onto the Largs branch. It is still used by EMUs on ECS moves to/from Ardrossan and Largs. (October 1979)

*Left*: A six-car set departs Annbank Junction heading towards Mauchline with the 'Ayrshire Wanderer' railtour, which had just reversed off the Killoch Branch, seen to the right. (October 1982)

A six-car set passes Barassie signal box with a Central to Ayr service. Note on the left the Troon Avoiding Lines, sadly gone, although some sidings remain for freight services to reverse. (June 1979)

A three-car set at Prestwick with an Ayr to Central working, 51014 leading. This station was renamed Prestwick Town in 1994 to distinguish it from Prestwick International Airport station a mile further north. (November 1979)

A three-car set at Dumfries with the 09.10 Ayr to Carlisle service, 51038 leading. This was up there with my best journeys on the 126s. (December 1979)

A six-car set at the entrance to Killoch Colliery with the SDPS's 'Ayrshire Wanderer' railtour. (October 1982/Angus Ross)

51009 inside Polmadie Depot getting its gangway vestibule removed. Drivers had complained for years about the draughts and by the late 1970s ASLEF were threatening industrial action. (May 1979/Angus Ross)

A three-car set passes Hillhouse Junction east of Barassie with the 09.10 Ayr to Carlisle service, 51048 leading. The line on the left led to Hillhouse Quarry but this traffic ceased in 2001. (December 1979)

A six-car set crosses Dalrymple Viaduct on the Chalmerston Branch heading south with the 'Ayrshire Wanderer' railtour. Sadly coal traffic ceased in 2010 and it has been mothballed since, although the track is still on site but very overgrown. (October 1982)

A six-car set passes Bogside signal box with a Central to Girvan service. A new large housing development has been built in the area beyond the signal box, but Transport Scotland do not seem to be interested in reopening this station. (September 1980)

A six-car set passes Glasgow Central Signalling Centre with a service from Ayr, 51045 leading. This centre closed in 2016 and work was transferred to the West of Scotland Signalling Centre at Cowlairs. (August 1980)

A three-car set approaches Irvine with a Central to Ayr service, 51032 leading. (October 1980)

A six-car set at Monkton with a Central to Ayr service. The adjacent sidings are still used by aviation trains. (November 1980)

A three-car set arrives at Maybole with a Central to Girvan service, 51042 leading. The line between Dalrymple Junction and Girvan was singled in 1974. (August 1981)

*Above*: A three-car set departs Stranraer Harbour with the 21.25 service to Glasgow Central. This shot was taken just before the blue livery started to be replaced by the blue and white colours. (July 1977/Paul Strathdee)

*Right*: A six-car set with a DMSL leading arrives at the old Central platform 12. One of my early shots but it does show the headcode 1A10. I remember it arriving at 18.20 to form the 18.35 service back to Ayr. (August 1975)

Ayr when the 126s ruled supreme. On platform 3 a three-car set has arrived on a local from Girvan. In platform 2 a six-car set gets ready for a departure to Central and a six-car 101 awaits its next work in platform 1. More 126s can just be seen in Kyle Street adjacent to the station. (November 1980)

An Ayrshire three-car set in Princes Street Gardens with an Edinburgh to Glasgow Central via Shotts service. The booked 107 had failed and the 126 stepped up. (April 1981/David Kay)

*Above*: Three-car failure lying in Irvine East Yard. It was believed to have engine problems and was shunted off the main line. This line behind the camera continued to Kilmarnock via Dreghorn and Crosshouse but was closed by Dr Beeching in April 1964. This area is now all gone, being replaced by a Tesco superstore and other retail outlets from the late 1990s. (July 1982)

*Right*: A six-car set passes Elderslie No. 1 signal box with a Central-Ayr service, 51039 leading. Note the mineral wagons parked up behind the box. These were used to and from the old coal depot at Paisley Canal yard. (July 1979)

A three-car set at Irvine with a Central to Ayr service. The station canopy was replaced by a glass entrance as part of the upgrading during electrification work in 1986. (October 1979)

Glasgow Central with various 126 units. On the left a six-car set works the 15.35 to Girvan and on the right a six-car set has just arrived from Stranraer Harbour. (August 1981)

A six-car set at Hunterston Junction takes the connecting spur to the Low Level Terminal. This was working the 'Ayrshire Wanderer' railtour. (October 1982)

51015 inside Glasgow Works. It had been in for a classified repair, probably its last. Note the end gangway had already been sealed up. (March 1981/David Kay)

Three-car set passes Elderslie No. 1 signal box with a Central to Ayr working. The sidings on both sides are long gone and the useful diversionary connection onto the Paisley Canal branch history. Attempts to reinstate the station have been met with no interest from Transport Scotland. (July 1979)

A three-car set at Barassie with an Ayr to Central service, with 51037 trailing. Note the railman. Barassie, like certain other stations in Ayrshire, became unmanned from September 1986 upon electrification of the line. (November 1980)

A three-car set at West Kilbride with a Central to Largs service, with 51017 trailing. This line was singled in 1987 with a parallel freight line and the Glasgow bound platform removed. As a result severe congestion ensues whenever any disruption occurs. (October 1982)

A three-car set on the Troon Avoiding Line with a diverted Central to Ayr service, 51043 leading. Note the golfers nearby presumably searching for a ball. This useful line closed a few days after this picture was taken. (November 1982)

*Left*: Driver Davy Quinn of Ayr depot at the controls of 51020 on the 15.05 Stranraer Harbour to Central service near Irvine. Davy was full of the patter and an enjoyable journey ensued. (August 1981)

*Below*: The start of the Ayrshire withdrawals. Two ex-E&G cars, 79088 and 79479, lie at Falkland Yard. They were soon stripped and left the yard and headed to the scrap man later in the year. (August 1981)

A three-car set in the snow at Brownhill Junction south of Glengarnock with a Central to Ayr service. Note Glengarnock steelworks in the background and the Kilbarchan Flyover, which was closed in 1972. (December 1981)

A three-car set at Prestwick with a Central to Girvan service. Note the signal box in the background – long gone. The station also had a third platform on the left just beyond the bridge but the track was removed in the early 1970s. (May 1980)

A general view of Ayr Townhead Coal Yard before electrification. A couple of withdrawn 126s can already be seen awaiting their fate. (August 1981)

A three-car set approaches Irvine with an Ayr to Central service, 51036 leading. Note the 08 stabled in the West Yard behind the signal box and the Caperboard factory to the east. Sadly all gone and replaced by retail developments. (December 1981)

*Above*: A three-car set, with 51037 trailing, stabled in between duties at Corkerhill Depot. By this time the 126s were in the minority and did not havc long to go. (March 1982)

*Right*: A three-car set approaches Kilmarnock with the 10.35 ex-Stranraer Harbour. This working lasted until September 1982. A Class 37 sits in the middle road awaiting a path onto the single line to Lugton with a freight service. (March 1982)

A six-car set, with 51026 trailing, at Kilmacolm with another arrival from Glasgow Central. Ironically the 126s hardly worked over this line until near the end when the line was doomed to close. (November 1982)

A nine-car set at Bogside between Kilwinning and Irvine working the 17.12 Central to Ayr. This was known locally as the 'Bowler Hat Brigade' train due to the amount of city gents using it. Note how the trailer cars leant to one side because of the side compartments. (October 1979)

*Above*: A three-car set at Largs ready to depart with the 14.52 service to Central, 51043 trailing. A very wet day. Note the water running off the coach roof overflow pipes. (November 1982)

*Right*: A six-car set at Elderslie with an Ayr to Central service. Note the mini vans on flat wagons stabled on the right. They had been brought up from Dagenham and would be distributed from the nearby Linwood Factory site. (June 1982)

A six-car set just south of Irvine with a Glasgow Central to Girvan service, 51013 leading. The area to the right has been completely changed with a super Tesco dominating new retail outlets. (October 1979)

The class frequently visited Shields Depot for tyre turning. Taken from a passing 126, a three-car set can be seen in the yard with 51035 leading in amongst other traction. (August 1981)

A six-car set and a Class 40 at Dalry. The six-car set was working a Central to Ayr service and the 40 was running light to Ardrossan Town to pick up Mk1 stock for the Papal visit, which had taken place at Bellahouston Park in Glasgow. (June 1982)

One of the ex-E&G cars that ended up in Liberia, West Africa. This was after it had been involved in a level crossing crash with a lorry. (September 2009/Femi Tobias)

Four car crosses Campbells Brig Viaduct north of Irvine with a Central to Ayr service. Additional DMBS power car 51032 had been added to the formation possibly for a test. (June 1981)

A six-car set at Brownhill Junction signal box with a Girvan to Central service. This was a busy junction at one time. Note the grass area on the left – this is where the North Johnstone lines via Kilbarchan joined the main line. (June 1982)

A six-car set north of Irvine with the 11.15 Ayr to Central service, 51033 leading. (April 1982)

A six-car set at Elderslie with the 07.10 Ayr to Central, 51041 leading. Note the coal train heading south in the background. The third coach was 51017, which made it into preservation at Boness. (November 1980)

*Left*: A six-car set passes the village of Patna on the Chalmerston Branch with the 'Ayrshire Wanderer' railtour. Patna and various other towns on this route have been deprived of a passenger service since 1964. (October 1982)

*Below*: A three-car set arrives at Troon with an Ayr to Central service, 51046 leading. In 2021 the station buildings to the right were burnt down. They were rebuilt in 2024 in time for the Open Golf Championship. (July 1979)

A Class 26 loco departs from Falkland Yard, Ayr, with one of the many 126 convoy scrap workings, in this case as far as Carlisle Kingmoor Yard. It consisted of eight vehicles, mainly ex-power cars, and was routed via Annbank Junction and Mauchline. (June 1983)

Thornhill Sidings, north of Dumfries. These 126 coaches were amongst the first batches of withdrawals on their way to Snailwell in Cambridgeshire. The formations included 51047, 51030, 51010, 59391, 51023, 59403, 59409, 79470, 79088 and 51019, 51045, 59405, 51027, 51021, 51050, 51009, 51049, 59395. (April 1982)

Fitters at Dunfermline Townhill Depot start to remove the engines from 51026. Apparently they were taken to Haymarket Depot and fitted to a 101 set. I later travelled on Ayr services shortly after and recognised their dulcet tones! (April 1983)

51043 being lifted from the tracks at Laurencekirk Sidings onto a low loader and taken to the Caledonian Railway Group at Brechin. (July 1983)

Preserved unit 126413 set at Bridge of Dun. The DMSL coach 51017 nearest to the camera had a lucky life. It was involved in the 1973 Gower Street crash near Central but was at the front when an EMU struck its stablemates from the rear and in 1979 it was also involved in the Paisley Gilmour Street smash when 51031 leading to Central was destroyed; this time 51017 was at the rear. (February 1984)

All things come to an end. One of the ex-E&G cars that ended up in Liberia, West Africa. This was after it had been withdrawn from traffic and it was in a sorry state. There is a rumour that all the 126 coaches are now buried at a site near the mining area. (September 2009/Femi Tobias)

An internal view in trailer coach SC 59404 at Bo'ness showing part of a first-class compartment. Impressive is an understatement. (June 2014)

The preserved three-car 126 at Boness. A fantastic job was done by all. (August 2010)